HELLO,
STRANGER

HELLO, STRANGER

BEACH POEMS

ROBERT DANA

ANHINGA PRESS
1 9 9 6

This is the first time Robert Dana's beach poems
have been published as a single volume.
The author thanks the editors of the following
magazines in which these poems first appeared:
*The Antioch Review, High Plains Literary Review,
The Iowa Review, Manoa, National Forum, Poetry Now,
Ploughshares, Shenandoah, The Southern California
Anthology,* and *The Wallace Stevens Journal.*

Library of Congress Cataloging in Publication Data
Dana, Robert
Hello, Stranger

I. Title
Library of Congress Catalog Card Number
96-83496, ISBN: 0-938078-43-7

Printed in the United States of America
First Edition: March 1996

Anhinga Press, Inc. is a nonprofit corporation staffed
by volunteers and dedicated wholly to the publica-
tion and appreciation of fine poetry.

To beach rats everywhere

CONTENTS

AUTHOR'S NOTE

Beaches have always had a special resonance for me, both personally and as a writer. They are my soul country.

Perhaps this is because the only moments of intense happiness I remember from my Depression childhood—in the years before my mother died and the world fell apart—are moments on a hot sandy beach, followed by images of sunburn and blueberries and poison ivy. I also recall the dark flavor of tinned sardines eaten whole on saltines under shady trees on the village green of some little Cape Cod town. My accomplice was a childhood acquaintance I never saw again after that summer—a boy with a charge account at the general store. Mostly I remember the wicked brightness of the sea under the sun—that small moment of peace.

How we came to be there in a cottage on the Cape—my mother, my sister, and I—is still unclear in the family story, in which so much is blurred or erased or forgotten. Apparently, someone made my mother the present of a couple of weeks there. We had little money, so it had to be something like that.

On the other hand, perhaps my feeling for the beach and the sea has to do with the genes I have from my Irish, ship-captain grandfather. He sailed first out of Cork at the turn of the century, and later out of Boston. I never knew him, and I carry no distinct memory of his face, or of a single sea-story he ever told—a fact I'm very sorry for. Another kind of Depression deprivation. But Irishness has its mysterious ways, and patterns of knowing and feeling get transmitted willy-nilly on the wind.

One thing is certain. Where sea meets shore marks the margin where the whole of this world meets: earth, water, sky; fire and light and darkness; the human and the bestial; young and old; rich and poor; the rooted, the rootless; the living and the dead. It's the most democratic place on earth.

rpd

November 20, 1995
Coralville, Iowa

CAPE
COD

NOW

You come over a hill, suddenly,
late afternoon or early evening
on 6A to Beach Point. Provincetown
to Long Point Light, a yellow,
dissolving Venice by Whistler
or Monet. Bay flat. Silver
grey. Dark blue further out.
I'm not talking about the past.
I'm talking about my sister,
my wife, myself,—all of us
travelling without reservations.
I'm talking about three small
sails tacked on the far horizon.
At Shoreline Village, cabins
1930's, sixty bucks a night
and twenty yards from salt water,
my sister talks about shells.
Sister Whine. Sister Twinkle.
Fifty years a nun this spring
and all No to my Yes. A taste
for dull food, and expensive
Irish whiskey in her tea. Next
door, our neighbors play volley
ball without a net, their little
girls shrieking like sea-birds.
Danielle. Michelle. Julie.
I'm not talking about childhood.
I'm saying when the tide here
goes out its long mile at dusk,
the bay's a wet barnyard where
a dozen boats strand and heel over,
and clammers rake the golden muck
for steamers. Later, the years

come down slowly like stars
on Mama's West Dennis or Harwich
or wherever we summered the fall
she died, hundreds of herring-fry
shoaling and sparkling in a bright
terror of shallows, my sister's
beads clicking in the night. I'm
not talking now about memory,
but the way words leap backward
to their beginnings, Wittgenstein's
"significant silences," his desk
drawer of posthumous phrases,
words detached into mystery
on little scraps of blue paper.
So the clear argument of morning
comes on, and lovers rise
from their rented beds to lie
in the sun. In Commercial Street,
one man receives from another
"the signature of God" in his hand.
"What is it?" I ask my wife.
A talisman? A smooth stone?
A word from Hebrew cast in silver?
I lay back on the sand of this
rough prayer of a beach and close
my eyes on the four white ribs
of the sky, listening to the low
roll of surf say *"jour,"* *"jour,"*
and sometimes *"toujours"* to the shore.

1986

THESE DAYS

I don't stay in town long.
I drive out to Race Point,—
bright stunt kites, diving
and sailing in the stiff, north
wind, and people walking
the beach. The sea's sunny
and dark. I drive on, down
to Herring Cove, park,
and walk the beach myself.
A man and woman are fishing.
"What do you catch here?"
I ask. "Blues," the man
says. "Bass sometimes,
but mostly blues," he says.
"How's the fishing been?"
"Good," the woman says.
"We was down Whaddyacallit?
—Highland? High Point.
A guy had five blues. Big."
Her hands measure off four
feet of air. "Well, good
luck," I say, and move on.
It's the end of the season,
and back at East Harbor—
if I write this in French,
will it be clearer? In Spanish,
will it be more passionate?
You're reading a translation.
The beach is empty. High
cirrus and a scrap of lemon
on blue sky, and salt-grass

Thoreau named *psamma arenaria*
for its love of sand when
Nauset was desert. I'm swirling
my wind-chilled whiskey
in its glass, and watching the sun
collapse in heaven-fire,
or wild glory, or whatever
passes for that these days.

1989

TOPSAIL ISLAND

AQUAMARINE

Downrange from LeJeune,
gutted missile tracking
towers; hints of cordite
and jet-fuel on the sea-
wind. North Topsail's
mile-wide strip of old
government issue bleached
the color of summer chino.
Beach a flat, brown bake
at ninety-eight degrees.
We shell before breakfast,
washing the morning's haul
in the kitchen sink. Dull
Atlantic cockles mostly;
a Baby's Ear; one perfect
Lion's Paw; a few, small,
bright calicoes my sister
wouldn't walk so far for,
just as she won't sketch
swimmers, or the jeweled hues
of the blue crab I hold up
for her by one of its fire-
tipped claws, or recall
from deep space the years
before my mother's death,
the voice I can't remember.
"Those weren't nice times,"
she says. I stand there,
looking out over the sea,
listening to the surf's white,
ruffled, incessant hush;

thinking how, in a few
days, a surgeon will open
my throat for the second
time in three years and
make me wise, if plastic
tubing carrying away
the body's dark fluids,
or drugged grief is wisdom.
This morning, I'm brave
and dumb as those young
chopper jocks we watched
last night, practicing
blind landings from the
carrier moored off shore.
Dumb as sunlight on these
red and yellow umbrellas,
or the waves that wrap
the pale shoulders of my
beautiful, young wife in
a gown of shining froth.

1988

RAPTURE

In the thick, Carolina night,
the great luggage of the sea
falls thudding and trundling
and tumbling up the stairs of
beach; its undertow hissing,
sometimes spitting, rolling
back on its own prolonged
susurrations; pouring in
loud hushes across planking
through the open bedroom door;
flooding room and mirror;
overwhelming our breathing;
drowning, almost, even sleep
in which something deeper
hurries away, and the day
repeats and repeats itself
like the heaven of the waves,
and we waken again to thrum
of diesel and the raging sun.

1993

HELLO, STRANGER

We have sea today—
fetch, chop, roller, wave;
a gun-metal green
Atlantic breaking up
along the October shore,
its surf exploding in
a rush of struck crystal—
not a generalization.
And how shall we place
the prints of gulls, whip
and snout, squadroned
stingray in the sand;
the ghost crab's fine
tattooing; bushels of
broken shell that yield
one perfect scallop
rayed red, red-orange
as this morning's sun?
Such categories make
up our great fiction,
the lie, the excuse
by which we forgive our-
selves the mysteries
of the particular—
this waking day, the
broken acropolis of

McKee's pier shipping
its usual eight feet
of salt water; some-
one's sand-printed
"Hello, stranger," fading
in the brisk sou'wester.

1993

STARS

Northeast of Hatteras
the great hurricane dawdles
and wheels, winding the sea
clock-spring tight; wave
piling against raging wave
two hundred miles out;
causing the tidal surge
to break on our beach here
in rips and chunks. Over-
head, Scorpio and Aquila
and The Serpent Bearer,
and a half billion stars
glitter like plankton.

*

Along the high backs
of the dunes, sea oats,
wild morning glories,
root and spread and hold.
And the kite leaves my
hand easily, rising
on the wind like a thing
of the spirit; a soul;
breath in a sky-full
of clouds and blue.
A Winslow Homer day.
Faces that all turn
away from you, toward
the sea, the sky, some-
thing far distant,
out of the picture.

Our Shrimp Lady's gone
who used to sit beside
the tailgate of her pick-
up on a patch of sandy
shoulder along 210.
"Only an hour out
of the water," she'd say,
scooping handsful of shrimp
from her Igloo cooler
into the pan of a hanging
scale—all sizes, heads
on, pink, glistening.
$5.50 a pound. Her knotted
fingers counting you back
the exact, odd change
from an old cigar box.
Ahead of us yesterday
at The Food Lion,
a man paid with food
stamps. "Have a nice
day," the checkout lady
said. "Sure will.
Is there any other kind?"

Is there any other kind?

            *

Starlette C. Carr. Star-
lit sea. Age 9. Buried
in that piece of trash
ground back there among

the pulp pines. Little
black girl. Little white
girl. Doesn't matter
in that pauper's field
where the only other
stone lies set in sand;
the graves of the other
ordinary dead marked
only by 3 x 5 cards
in metal holders stuck
in the earth; names,
dates, fading in sun
and rain. Plates like
those designed for labeling
roses in formal gardens:
Starlit Sea. Starlet.
This car-stopping
display—stars, hearts—
all arranged on stands,
a pink phone resting
on the pages of an open
telephone directory,
waiting a call from heaven—
were fresh a week ago.
Now, they're slumped
to the look of melted
ice cream at a ruined
summer party. Shall
I try to dial her number?
"Starlette, honey? Star."
shall I say? and ask her

when she's coming home?
What little good we do
here, standing in this
soft, southern drizzle,
we do, like parents,
for love, for the living.

1995

FORT MYERS BEACH

ESTÉRO ISLAND BEACH CLUB

By day, they lie
beside the heated,
turquoise pools,
tanning to the look
of imported leather;
at evening, gathering
beachside on the terrace
to celebrate a sun
going down gold off
Sanibel and Captiva.
Businessmen, retired
farmers and their wives,
bearing a eucharist
of chips and dip;
nachos smothered
in Wisconsin cheddar;
olives of California
cardboard packed
in water. Booze
for the blood of Christ.
They talk mostly
of money, reckoned
in hundred thousands;
of acres of land;
plats, accesses;
strings of hot-dog
stands; the old
joke about the guy
who puts a twenty

in the collection plate
and takes out change.
Back in Illinois,
the farmhouse is modern.
No longer the flaking
shit-kicker cold
enough in winter
away from the wood-
burning stove to stop
your breath; in summer,
muggy as a sponge,
and smelling sickly
sweet of peonied
wallpapers, milk,
and manure. Behind
the barn, the White
Diamond silo tilts
in the air like
something Italian;
the colors of early
spring are Tuscan—
umber and ochre
under a breath of slip.
Hours later, passing
two vagrant kids

sleeping on a stolen
blanket, I'll still
hear them, these
voices raw-tongued
and democratic,
speaking without apology;
and the moon will rise
silvery over a talc
and powdered sugar
beach, and the Gulf
breeze strike softly
across the bright
praise of waters.

1989

FLORIDIANA

Like a drunk off curbstone
or a cow off a flat rock,
all day rain pisses down;
wind turning the Gulf
yellow-grey; the islands
to the north, disappearing.
In the parking lot at Winn
Dixie, one man's kicking
the shit out of another—
fists and feet, brother.
The lost, the venereal;
living, if you can call
it that, out of a rust-
bucket van under sabal
palms; come to the end
of something Floridian.
Why lie about it? The day
is vicious or indifferent.
The voices of the lawyer-
poets and tennis-poets and
landlord-poets are so much
bleached and broken shell
here; so many red and
pink stars of hibiscus
in green heavens of hedge.
All night I dream dream
after dream of this; until
the rain stops and pale
morning comes and I waken
to a boy's voice on my phone;
a former student looking

for work in frigid Minneapolis.
And I'm listening—the door
to the room open—and I'm
watching two white terns,
close to shore, striking—
first, one; then, the other—
striking again and again,
cold sparks on the water.
I can taste the sharp salt,
and hear the boy's voice
talking on and on and on.

1992

OFF DAY ON ESTÉRO

Scuzzy, grey bay waters
to the horizon, and the
low breakers' monotonous
wash. A groundskeeper
saying, "I got a cousin
take a black snake or
copperhead by the tail
an' snap it, ya' know?"
He whips his right wrist
downward. "Breaks their
necks. Makes nice belts
an' hatbands out of 'em."
Down toward Anthony's
Sunset-By-The-Sea,
nine black pilings rot
with infinite patience
where sea burns shore;
atop three, three
cormorants hold out
their sodden, black
wings to dry; heraldic
triangle; ensign
of some shadow cabinet
in exile, stamped on air.
Here, on the terrace
above the beach, palm
fronds float like *voladores*
on the wind; and the children
feed the frenzied gulls,
and taming them, turn
them vicious. So that,

finally, you pray hard
for Sunday. For sun.
And the young men
loud in their perfect
arrogance. And their
girls, their walking
an unconscious music,
next to naked in their
terrifying beauty.

1994

HOW TO MAKE A GOOD GREEN SOUP

First, peel and seed
and chop four cucumbers
coarsely, paying strict
attention to the clack
of shuffleboard discs
and the shouts of four
small boys below your
sunny screen porch.
There is, of course, the
steady white rush
of the wind-beaten sea;
and, if you close your
eyes, the blowing palm
fronds may make you
think you hear rain,
or water dribbling
in a nearby fountain.
Next, chop two large
scallions, and seed
and chop one small,
dark green jalapeño.
Test a small slice
and feel its heat

buzz immediately
across your tongue
and lips like nothing
electrical. Do not
rub your eyes. By now,
the boys' voices have
become those of old
men at horseshoes
in the sand, and the clang
of ringers and leaners.
Chop, again coarsely,
a good half cup
of cilantro leaves,
until the little kitchen
of your fingers fills
with its sweaty pungence.
Combine it all
in the blender with
two cups of butter-
milk, a little lemon
juice, and a pinch
of salt; then, put it
in the fridge to chill.
Down beach, there's
only one cormorant
this year on the black
pilings, and the young
friends who honey-
mooned here have
already divorced.
This morning, as I

jogged the beach,
I saw a woman
in her yard watering
a young palm. She
wore blue shorts and
a soft, grey, long-
sleeved, collarless
cotton shirt and moved
carefully around it
with her green hose.
She was no longer
young, but she'd
been someone's pretty
girl once. And then
I thought about this
good green soup,
topped with small,
pink shrimp freshly
boiled and peeled,
and how I'd make it.

1995

THE SALAMANDER

It can hold its place
on the baked concrete
terrace for a solid
hour without moving
even its bird-bright
eye. Everything
about it in motion:
the slow, fierce sun,
strollers on the beach,
bathers and sunbathers,
the lapping surf,
the wind, the palms
feathering overhead,
the gulls and pelicans
flapping and gliding.
Its only intention
seems to be to be
there, a comma, a late
refinement in the white
grammar of afternoon.

1995

THE GILL NETTERS

An odd one. A kind of sea-
going john-boat. Twenty
feet long and Navy grey.
Maybe an eight- or nine-foot
beam. Very shallow draft
to work that close to shore.
And no cockpit. Instead,
a kind of narrow conning
tower open to the weather.
Up there, her skipper sits
hatless, in an orange slicker
working throttle and wheel
and wireless phone. No
name lettered astern. No
My Money or Sea Queen or Wet
Dreams. No port of origin.
Just a row of plain black
numbers stencilled on her bow.

The morning's cold rains had
tailed off, leaving the Gulf
sky, the sand, the water all
a marly agate. Then we saw
her anchor-buoy a yard off
shore like a lost basketball;
the boat awash in a trough
behind the sandbar; lengths
of net paying out across her
transom through the hands
of two men in yellow slicker
pants held up by braces. One,

moustached; one under a red,
billed cap. Both strong
armed and sun-dark. Cubans,
maybe. Francisco. Manuel.
Patiently setting a double
coil, a weir, a labyrinth of
perhaps a hundred yards of
clear monofilament, its rosary
of cork floats riding the swells.

There's wind, of course, light
now, and South-southwest—up
from Havana and the Keys—and
a few last spits of rain.
"Time spent fishing cannot
be deducted from a man's soul,"
someone said. Tell that to the
dolphins cruising the sandbar
for strays, turning the water
white with their sudden rushes,
their instincts sure as sharks'.
I think these men are brothers
—Manos. Francisco. Fingers
cut and stinging—*Chinga tu madre!*
—shoulders cramping—brothers
in the salt stink and sweat
of hauling and picking. Mullet
are saved; the trash fish tossed
to two pelicans bobbing astern.
And, finally, in the last few
yards of net, a stingray—

a good three feet, wing-tip
to wing-tip, its dark tail
wicked as a cane, is flipped
into the grey-green water,
as the boat sidles and yaws,
its screws barely turning.
"God, is it still alive?"
a woman standing next to me
says to no one in particular.
But there's no way to know
at this distance—what is it?
thirty yards? Then the boat
kicks up a wake and heads
for harbor. The crowd of sno-birds
gathered to watch disperses
slowly, murmuring. No way
to know. Not then. Not now.

1995

& ELSEWHERE

YOU

When I think
of the simple
fact of you
walking there,
I see the coming
on of long red-
gold afternoons
over the sea;
the long, even
longer evenings;
blue-purple and
black-green skies
going down
in a slow, silver
sweat of stars
on the Gulf of Mexico.

1988

NASSAU: PRINCE GEORGE'S WHARF

She points.
Jesús gaffs the yellowtail
from the live box,

nails its head
to the cutting board

and with four quick
strokes of his long,
flexible, blunt knife

guts, gills, and bones it.

Three rags,
three pennants of bright meat

he drops
into a brown paper bag.

She pays him
in paper and silver.

She will cook tonight
over charcoal,
with herbs and lemon.

Tomorrow,
beside this same boat,
the sun will school again

on the water.

1978

KEY WEST: LOOKING FOR HEMINGWAY

On Mallory Docks
the kids applaud
when the sun goes down

Women
in the hot splash of Key West print

Cayo Hueso

where the light gathers
thick enough to breathe

And up at Southernmost
in his air-conditioned room
an off-duty cop sprawls

cooling
in the bruised blue art of his tattoos
veins shot full of lye

The look of the eyes
you would remember Papa

And the yellow rice
and the black beans and Cuban bread
at the Miramar

Standing here
knee-deep in the shallows
watching the small wahoo holding steady

ghost-fish

I think of you
with your forehead smashed
into perfect prose

plumbing the blue gulf of the Gulf

Behind the *Pilar*
the marlin
breaks water like a great angel

shaking from its sail
a halo of sun-struck brine

And I call out
silently

in a voice you cannot hear

into that terrible
that clear emptiness

where you were

1978

BAD HEART

So you walk along nowhere—
anybody's beach—the air
a rank chowder of low tide
and you're happy. You'd like
to sew yourself a shirt
out of sunlight. You want
to tell your wife you love
her. And you wait for the
telephone in your ear to ring—.
For an hour. For a week. Is
abstraction a net or a sieve,
Angel? Is an idea a kiss?
A shape such as maples
make unfurling, or willows
falling? Or a steady river
taking up silt and stone,
showing you in a knot or curl,
depth and speed of channel.

And what does it show
if a boat-tail still rudders
in the bucking cross-wind of
your head, where you put it
one green middle-western
afternoon ten years ago,
when you were younger,
and she was very young?

1983

ON THE PUBLIC BEACH, ST. AUGUSTINE

Sanderlings. Turnstones. A lone
Willet. Fog-colors morning
sun hasn't yet cut through.
The still cold, grey-green March
Atlantic rolling shoreward flank
after glassy flank. Fraying,
plunging, flattening in its final
scouring rush, to salty lager.
Our old *Sylvan*'s gone, with its
blue-shuttered, wind-scrubbed
weekend cabins. Its tiny
kitchenettes. Wind-white
bedsheets rich with the whiff
of something healing. The quick,
illimitable light. Bulldozed
out for a squat of brown condos.
But the beach is still the public
beach we remember. And we follow
its straggling tidelines like kids,
picking among the strew of broken
arks and angel wings and razors.
The sun lags. But I can't wait
to wade out on the water's
electric chill. The skin buzzes.
The young shine like seraphim
just stepped from their clothes.
Remember how each brisk, incoming
breaker caught our breaths
and lifted us to our toes,

until we took a wet shoulder
and rode it in? Up the beach,
somebody's dog barks like heaven,
flinging itself for joy over
the live backs of the waves.
We laugh, and our talk dwindles
to held hands, as if we perceived,
in body, these things, immediate
and whole. As if we lived, as pure
mathematicians say, on a set
of measure zero, where anything
might happen. At Matanzas, south
of here, *jubilatio* at noon:
shrimp fresh-steamed to crispness
at King's Bait, and eaten from
a plastic cup, their tails tossed
to the complaining gulls. As if
far out from shore, four pelicans
might coast, perfectly echeloned,
long crests and spills of light.
The last time we came here,
in '79, Hurly'd just killed
himself, blown his head open,
back in Iowa, with his god-
damned Smith & Wesson,
the brown corn-stubble essing
easy over the winter hills
like the ancient Chinese character
for river. Now, I no longer
believe we return as birds or fish
or even grit on the heave of the wind.

I think we were never anything
but what we are: the last, lovely,
complex turn of it. And like
this planet, once, and for one
time only. Inventors of this
sea of cloud-struck afternoons,
of heat-haze, the happy dog
of the waves—walking at sun-up
with other strangers this flat
reach of sand, and smiling
occasionally, back at them
as they pass. Saying, occasionally,
"Good morning. Good morning."

1986

YOU TELL ME

We've been told this beach
is dangerous—Oyster Bay,
where the sun sets in the east,
and the Indian Ocean's thick
as chicken soup, and warm,
and only the evening wind
on your wet skin refreshes—
a jogging ambassador mugged
here, twice, by roving gangs;
once for his pair of Nikes.
So why have we come? To slip
the silences of compound
walls; the windows scrolled
in heavy iron? Or maybe
to watch the little party
of French, keeping their own
counsel, their bottle of wine
cooking in the African sun.
Or to swim with the Russians—
men stout-chested as trees,
kids diving and falling
continuously from their branches
into the cloudy water. Under
the chattering palm-fronds,
a half-dozen Tanzanian boys
drift from site to abandoned
site, eyeing the sand for
a comb, a scrap of bread,
a forgotten sock. Speechless.
Too proud to be seen among
the dusty Hondas and Peugeots.

Arab families, Pakistanis,
spread out on the breezy
dunes; for whom dusk pours
itself on the sea, a swath
of sari, silver and pink,
wafting out and out, all
the way, perhaps, to Chitta-
gong or Bombay. Perhaps
this is peace; or the salt
that makes up sweet truth;
or god, that hard syllable
on the dark lip of the world.
You know. You tell me.

Dar-es-Salaam, 1991

About the Author

Robert Dana was born in Boston in 1929, and has lived in Iowa for many years. He recently retired as Poet-in-Residence at Cornell College. The author of ten books of poetry, he has served as distinguished visiting poet at five universities and was awarded National Endowment Fellowships in poetry in 1985 and 1993. Mr. Dana's work won The Delmore Schwartz Memorial Award for poetry in 1989.

*Cover Art, Book Design and Production by David Wilder/***alt.image**

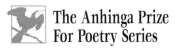 **The Anhinga Prize For Poetry Series**

Easter Vigil
by Ann Neelon, 1995
Joy Harjo/Judge

Mass for the Grace of a Happy Death
Frank X. Gaspar, 1994
Joy Harjo/Judge

The Physicist at the Mall
Janet Holmes, 1993
Joy Harjo/Judge

Hat Dancer Blue
Earl S. Braggs, 1992
Marvin Bell/Judge

Hands
Jean Monahan, 1991
Donald Hall/Judge

Other Books From Anhinga Press

Unspeakable Strangers
Van K. Brock, 1995

Isle of Flowers: *Poems by Florida's Individual Artist Fellows*
Long, Wallace, Campbell, eds, 1995

The Secret Life of Moles
P.V. LeForge, 1992

PS 3554 .A5 H45 1996
Dana, Robert, 1929-
Hello stranger

DATE DUE
